KS2
Success

REVISION GUIDE

Grammar, Punctuation and Spelling

Rachel Axten-Higgs

Contents

Grammar

Punctuation

Spelling

Vocabulary

Nouns and pronouns

What are nouns?

A noun is a word that is used to name a person, place, animal or thing. There are four main types of nouns that you need to be familiar with:

- Common nouns
- Proper nouns
- Collective nouns
- Abstract nouns

Common nouns

Common nouns are nouns that name a kind of person or thing. For example:

boy   day   sheep   laptop   school   house

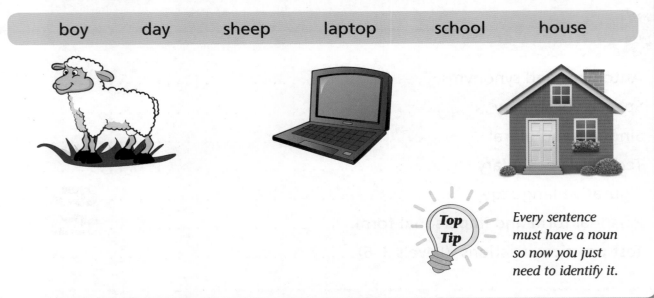

Top Tip

Every sentence must have a noun so now you just need to identify it.

Proper nouns

Proper nouns are nouns that refer to a particular place or person. They always start with a capital letter.

For example:

Freya   Europe   Chris   London

Collective nouns

Collective nouns are nouns that describe a group or collection of people or things. There are lots of different names for different groups. Here are some of the more common ones:

Crowd of people

Flock of birds

Herd of elephants

Bunch of flowers

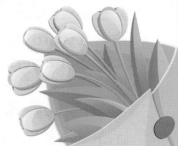

Abstract nouns

Abstract nouns are nouns that generally describe things that exist but cannot always be seen, heard, smelt, felt or tasted. For example:

sleep   hope   peace

What are pronouns?

A **pronoun** does the same job as a noun, but it can be used to refer to a noun, e.g. he, she, it, yours, they.

Mark was a sensible boy. **He** always listened to advice from **his** teachers.

Top Tip

Pronouns are great for preventing a piece of writing becoming too repetitive when the noun is continually being referred to. You can use pronouns to refer to the noun instead.

Key words

common noun

proper noun

collective noun

abstract noun

pronoun

Quick test

Which type of noun are these (common, proper, collective or abstract)?

1 Birmingham   *proper noun*

2 crowd   *collective*

3 elephant   *common*

4 trust   *abstract*

5 Claire   *proper*

Verbs and adverbs

What is a verb?

A **verb** is a word that describes an action or state of being. Every sentence must contain a verb otherwise it is not a sentence.

> The boy cried loudly.
>
> The word **cried** is the verb.

> The children played happily.
>
> The word **played** is the verb.

> The first singer was clearly the best.
>
> The word **was** is the verb.

> The boat swayed.
>
> The word **swayed** is the verb.

 **Top Tip**

Auxiliary verbs *are the verbs* be, do, have, will, *when they are followed by another verb (the full verb), e.g. 'The boy* will eat *the pudding'.*

Verb tenses

A verb can change the **tense** of a sentence to show whether the event happens in the **past**, **present** or **future**.

PAST	PRESENT	FUTURE
The boy **ate** the pudding.	The boy **is eating** the pudding.	The boy **will eat** the pudding.

What are adverbs?

An **adverb** is a word that describes the verb (it gives extra information about the way in which the verb is happening). Adverbs can help to create a detailed picture in your reader's mind about what is happening. They can dramatically change the way that the verb is performed.

For example:

The girl visited the dentist.	The girl **reluctantly** visited the dentist.
The baby cried.	The baby cried **loudly**.
The dog barked	The dog barked **frantically**.

Adverbs describing adjectives

Adverbs can also be used to give extra information about an adjective.

The dress was ruined.	The dress was **completely** ruined.

The adverbs tested at Levels 3–5 will usually end with the letters 'ly'.

Top Tip

It is important not to overuse adverbs in your writing, but they can add detail for your reader if used sparingly.

Top Tip

Key words

verb

tense

past

present

future

adverb

Quick test

What tense are the verbs in these sentences?

1. The dog ran happily through the fields.
2. The snail is slithering along the path.
3. The children enjoyed their school visit.
4. The man is going to be late for his train.

Adjectives

What are adjectives?

Adjectives are describing words and are used to describe the noun in a sentence. Adjectives make your writing more interesting for your reader because they help to create a more vivid mental picture.

> The man sat on the bench.
> The **huge** man sat on the **small**, **wooden** bench.

> The house sat at the top of the hill.
> The **old**, **dark** house sat at the top of the **steep** hill.

Top Tip

When reading, make a note of adjectives that give you (as the reader) a vivid picture in your head. You can then use these exciting adjectives in your writing.

Comparative adjectives

Comparative adjectives are used to compare two nouns in a sentence to show that one noun is different in some way from the other, e.g. bigger, better, taller, shorter, etc. These adjectives usually end in 'er', unless the adjective has more than two syllables, in which case the word 'more' is used.

Chris is **bigger** than Freya.

Heena is **shorter** than Xavier.

Mark's bark is **more impressive** than Matilda's squeak.

| Matilda | Freya | Mark | Heena | Chris | Xavier |

Superlative adjectives

Superlative adjectives are used to show that one noun is different from all the others, e.g. tallest, shortest, the best, the worst, etc. These adjective usually end in 'est'. The words 'most' and least' are used for adjectives that have two or more syllables (and don't end in -y), e.g. honest – most honest; modern – most modern.

| Splodge | Dodge | Bodge | Plodge | Modge |

Modge is the **ugliest** monster in the row.

Splodge is the **prettiest** monster in the row.

Bodge is the **most charming** monster in the row.

Using effective adjectives

Sometimes it is easy to get into the habit of using the same adjectives in your writing. This can make it very dull for your reader.

> The **nice** boy sat on the **nice** bench and ate his **nice** ice-cream.

This sentence is not very exciting and it will not create a detailed picture for the reader. However, now look at this sentence:

> The **contented** boy sat on the **colourful** bench and ate his **delicious** ice-cream.

This sentence gives the reader much more information to form an interesting picture in their head.

Key words

adjective

comparative adjective

superlative adjective

Quick test

Underline the adjective and identify which type it is (adjective, comparative or superlative).

1. Heidi is the fastest runner in the school.

2. It was a beautiful day.

3. Jacob is slower than Chan at settling to work.

4. The soft snow was glittering on the path.

Subject–verb agreement

What are subjects?

Subjects in sentences are 'who' or 'what' the sentence is about. They are usually nouns, pronouns, noun phrases or noun clauses.

> Where is my **bike**?

> The **mouse** ate the cheese.

> **Hayden** was playing on his computer.

> The **teacher** shouted loudly.

Top Tip

*You can easily find the subject of the sentence if you spot the verb. The subject is **who** or **what** is doing the verb.*

Types of subjects

Subjects in a sentence can either be **plural** (where this is more than one person or object) or **singular** (one person or object).

The examples in the box above are all singular subjects as they refer to one person or object. In the examples given here, the subjects are plural.

> The **children** played in the park.

> The **pencils** fell out of the pot.

Top Tip

*Plural subjects often (but **not** always) have an 's' at the end.*

Making verbs and subjects agree

All sentences must have a **verb**, which in turn relates to the **subject** of the sentence. The rules are different for **singular** and **plural** subjects, but they are quite easy to remember.

The rules are usually as follows:

- If the subject is **singular**, then the verb is also **singular**.

- If the subject is **plural**, then the verb is also **plural**.

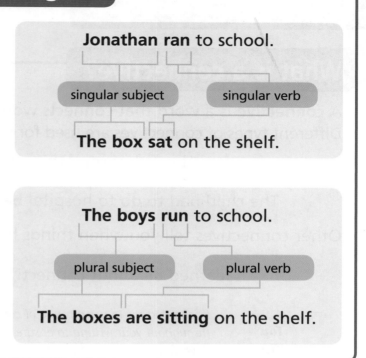

Jonathan ran to school.

| singular subject | singular verb |

The box sat on the shelf.

The boys run to school.

| plural subject | plural verb |

The boxes are sitting on the shelf.

Standard English

The term '**Standard English**' means correctly applying all of the rules of the English language when writing.

- Do not use slang in formal writing

- Make sure subjects and verbs agree

- Do not write how you would speak

- Check your work at the end

- Do not use double negatives

Top Tip

*Consider your **audience** (who you are writing for) and **purpose** (why you are writing) to determine how formal your writing needs to be.*

Common errors	Corrections
I ain't going.	I am not going.
I didn't say nothing.	I did not say anything.
I should of gone.	I should have gone.
The TV is broke	The television is broken.

Key words

verb

subject

singular

plural

Standard English

Quick test

Underline the subject and circle the verb in each sentence.

1. The letters were flying through the letterbox.

2. The letter flew through the letterbox.

Connectives

What is a connective?

A **connective** is a word that connects words, **phrases**, **clauses** and **sentences**. Different types of connectives are used for signalling different things in a sentence.

Some connectives show that something has been caused by something else:

> The child had to go to hospital **because** she bumped her head.

Other connectives tell you when things happened:

> I learned all about connectives **before** I ate my lunch.

Top Tip

It is important to use a range of connectives throughout your writing to ensure it is lively and flows for your reader. Connectives ensure that you don't have too many very short sentences.

Connectives for addition, sequencing, emphasising and comparing

Connectives can be used to add information to sentences in different ways.

- For addition:

> I like football **as well** as rugby.
>
> The water levels are rising, **moreover** we have run out of sand bags.

- For sequencing:

> Stick the eyes on **after** cutting the circle out.
>
> **Finally** after their long journey, they arrived at home.

- For emphasising:

> He loved animals **especially** the horses.
>
> The results were improving, **significantly** the maths ones.

- For comparing:

> The lion is a quiet animal **compared with** an elephant!
>
> He walks to school **in the same way** as a snail slithers along a path.

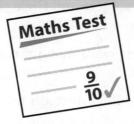

Maths Test

9/10 ✓

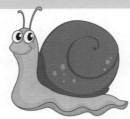

Connectives for co-ordinating, subordinating and contrasting

You can demonstrate higher skills in literacy by using connectives in even more ways to create a range of sentences. Connectives can sometimes be more than one word (e.g. 'for instance' or 'instead of' or 'as a result of').

- For co-ordinating:

> Maxwell went to the shop **and** bought the ingredients for his dinner.
>
> Tia likes reading **but** Samuel likes writing.

- For subordinating:

> The cat fell out of the tree **because** it was too heavy for the branch.
>
> We were in a lot of trouble and **as a result** had no pocket money.

- For contrasting:

> The children ran faster **although** they were tired.
>
> The paint had dried **unlike** the wallpaper.

Top Tip *If you try to use lots of different connectives, you will be using them to signal different things in the sentence, such as the cause or timing of an event.*

Key words

connective

phrase

clause

sentence

Quick test

Underline the connective in each sentence.

1. I bought an ice-cream because I was hungry.

2. Before the final whistle, the team scored the winning goal.

3. You need to come down from the roof otherwise you will fall!

4. The rain fell for days, as a result of this the pitch was flooded.

Types of sentence

Four main types

A **sentence** is a set of words that is complete in itself. It always contains a verb and usually a subject. There are four main types of sentence:

Make sure you use the correct punctuation to signal the type of sentence you are writing.

- A **statement** is a sentence that tells the reader something.

> Elephants are grey.

- A **question** is a sentence worded to find out information from the reader.

> What colour are elephants?

- A **command** is a sentence that tells the reader to do something.

> Go and wash that elephant.

- An **exclamation** is a sentence that contains a sudden cry or remark.

> That elephant is pink!

Simple sentences

A **simple** sentence (also called a **clause**) contains just one verb and one subject. It must make complete sense on its own and can take different forms, as outlined above.

> The chicken ran across the road.
>
> subject   verb

Compound sentences

A **compound** sentence is formed when two simple sentences (clauses) are joined together with a connective. Each of the clauses must make sense on their own before they are joined.

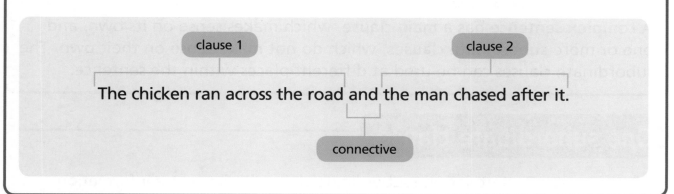

clause 1 | clause 2

The chicken ran across the road and the man chased after it.

connective

Complex sentences

A **complex** sentence has a **main clause** (which makes sense on its own) and one or more **subordinate clauses** (which do not make sense on their own).

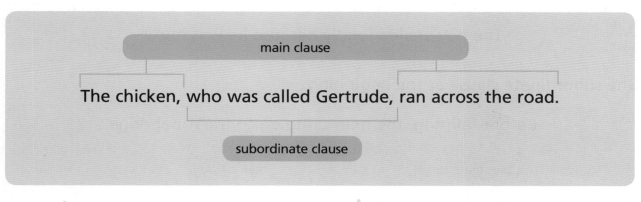

main clause

The chicken, who was called Gertrude, ran across the road.

subordinate clause

Top Tip

Vary your sentences throughout your writing so that it stays lively and interesting for your reader.

Top Tip

The most common subordinating conjunctions include: after, although, as, because, before, how, if, once, since, than, that, till, until, when, where, whether, while, who.

Key words

sentence	exclamation
statement	simple
question	compound
command	complex

Quick test

Add a subordinate clause to make these into complex sentences.

1. The lion roared loudly.

2. The children ran away.

3. The snow fell gently.

Complex sentences

Complex sentences

A **complex sentence** has a **main clause**, which makes sense on its own, and one or more **subordinate clauses**, which do not make sense on their own. The subordinate clauses can be used at different places within the sentence.

One subordinate clause

When a sentence contains one subordinate clause, it gives extra information about the main clause, either at the beginning, middle or end of the sentence.

One subordinate clause at the end:

The man clung on to the ropebridge before fainting.

main clause | subordinate clause

The boy wailed loudly because he was hurt.

One subordinate clause at the beginning:

Before fainting, the man clung on to the ropebridge.

subordinate clause | main clause

Because he was hurt, the boy wailed loudly.

One subordinate clause interrupting the main clause:

main clause

The man, before fainting, clung on to the ropebridge.

subordinate clause

The boy, because he was hurt, wailed loudly.

main clause

Two subordinate clauses

Sometimes a complex sentence can contain more than one subordinate clause, and the clauses give extra information about **two** different parts of the sentence. Again, each subordinate clause does not make sense on its own.

main clause

The man, who was terrified of heights, clung on to the ropebridge, before fainting.

1st subordinate clause	2nd subordinate clause

The boy, who was clumsy, wailed loudly, because he was hurt.

main clause

Top Tip

Try to use a range of complex sentences in your writing with a different number of clauses. This shows that you are able to control your writing.

Top Tip

Level 6

When subordinating clauses are used in the middle of a sentence, they usually use relative pronouns (e.g. who, which *or* that*). For example: The ducks, **who** were swimming in the pond, did not want to eat any more bread.*

Key words

complex sentence

main clause

subordinate clause

Quick test

Underline the **main clause** in these sentences.

1. Because they were cold, the children put their coats on.

2. The girl, who had red hair, climbed the steps of the slide.

3. The monkeys, who made a lot of noise, swung from the trees, because they were showing off.

4. After a very long drive, the family arrived at their destination!

5. Even though it was late, Harry walked to the shops as he wanted some chocolate.

Prepositions and articles

What is an article?

An **article** is a word that comes before a noun. In the English language there are only two types of articles:

- **Indefinite**
- **Definite**

There is only one definite article, which is   the .

The indefinite articles are   a   or   an .

For example:

> **An** apple is hanging on **the** tree.

> **The** umbrella has **a** handle.

The word 'an' is used before nouns that begin with a vowel (except some words beginning with 'u').

What are prepositions?

Prepositions are words that show the relationship of one noun or pronoun with another noun or pronoun.

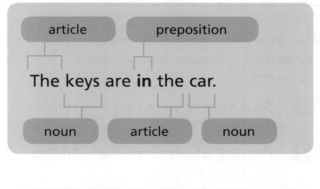

article   preposition

The keys are **in** the car.

noun   article   noun

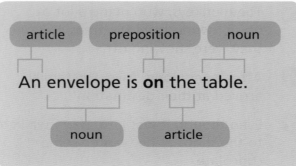

article   preposition   noun

An envelope is **on** the table.

noun   article

What are prepositions?

Here are some other examples of prepositions:

- The thief ran **along** the wall.
- Jake ran **past** the church.
- The athlete jumped **over** the hurdle.
- The girl swam **under** the water.
- Matilda slid **down** the slide.
- The hot air balloon flew **over** the city.

Check it makes sense

It is important to use the correct preposition to show the relationship of the two things to each other. If you use the wrong preposition, the sentence will not make sense.

For example, the following sentence does not make sense:

> Freya **ran above** the stairs.

Using a different preposition makes it more sensible:

> Freya ran **up / down** the stairs.

Key words

article

indefinite

definite

preposition

Quick test

Underline the preposition in each sentence.

1. The children were in the wardrobe.
2. The newspaper was on the table.
3. The dog ran into the butcher's shop.
4. The clouds floated above the buildings.
5. The cow jumped over the moon.

Paragraphs

What are paragraphs?

A **paragraph** is a set of sentences that are about an idea or a topic. They are used in longer pieces of writing to help the reader understand the settings, action and characters better.

There are no rules about the number of paragraphs needed in a piece of writing, or the number of sentences that must be in a paragraph.

Each paragraph should start with a **topic sentence**. The purpose of this sentence is to introduce the new information or change of direction (in a story). The paragraph should then develop the information from that sentence.

A new paragraph is normally used to indicate a change of time, person, event, new topic or speaker.

Developing topic sentences in non-fiction

A topic sentence states the main idea (or topic) of the paragraph. It should come at the start of the paragraph as it signals to your reader what the paragraph is about.

In non-fiction texts this topic sentence will be used to give a summary of the most important part of the paragraph.

For example, in a non-fiction book about the solar system, a paragraph about the planets might start with:

> There are 8 planets in our solar system.

However, it would not start:

> One of the planets in our solar system is called Mars and another one is called Neptune.

Lengths of paragraphs

In fiction texts, the paragraphs are used to signal new characters, places and actions, and they therefore can vary in length enormously.

A general guide is:

- A longer paragraph is used to slow the action down and to give lots of background information.

- A shorter paragraph is used when the action is moving quickly and the author is moving the story on at a pace.

Level 6

To help your paragraphs flow, you need to use the full range of cohesive devices. For example, pronouns (she, he), connectives (firstly, although), adverbs (slowly) and references to previous events.

Making links

It is important, in a piece of writing, to link the paragraphs together so that they are not seen as being independent of one another. This can be done by using linking words and phrases, e.g. 'then', 'after that', 'what happened next was important'.

Another way of doing this is through the connectives or references to previous events or future events. When planning your writing, make sure that you think about the paragraphs as signposts to lead your reader through – plan how you will link these to each other.

Key words

paragraph

topic sentence

Quick test

Look in your current reading book and note down the reasons for each change of paragraph.

Make a note of any linking words that are used and record them in your reading journals or notebooks for use in your own writing.

Tense agreement

Why are there different tenses?

The **tense** that a verb is written in tells the reader **when** the action happened. The three main tenses are:

- Past – it has already happened
- Present – it is happening now
- Future – it is going to happen

For example:

PAST The man **fell** out of the tree!	**PRESENT** The man **falls** out of the tree!	**FUTURE** The man **will fall** out of the tree!

Top Tip

Always look at the verb in the sentence to determine the tense.

Verb tables

Tables of verbs can help us to see how the verb changes in the three tenses as well as when different subjects are used.

For the verb '**to be**':

Subject	Present tense	Past tense	Future tense
I	am	was	will be
You	are	were	will be
He / She / It	is	was	will be
We	are	were	will be
They	are	were	will be

Top Tip

Say the sentence in your head to check it makes sense. You can quickly tell if you have used the wrong tense for the subject, e.g. 'We is..' cannot be correct!

Another tense

There is another tense (if you really want to show off your knowledge of grammar) – the **continuous** tense.

The continuous tense is used when the action is going on for some time (like building a house) rather than just a short action (like slamming a door).

For example, if you are staying in Spain for a week, this is how you would say it:

Present tense: **I stay** in Spain for a week's holiday.

Present continuous: **I am staying** in Spain for a week's holiday.

Past continuous: **I was staying** in Spain for a week's holiday.

There are different tenses for the verb '**to have**'.

Subject	Present	Past	Future	Present continuous	Past continuous
I	have	had	will have	am having	was having
You	have	had	will have	are having	were having
He / She / It	has	had	will have	is having	was having
We	have	had	will have	are having	were having
They	have	had	will have	are having	were having

Key words

tense

past

present

future

continuous

Quick test

Write down whether these sentences are in the past, present or future tense.

1. The dogs are going to race.
2. The cat is stealing the cream!
3. I enjoyed the visit.
4. I eat chocolate.
5. I cried all day!

Active and passive voice

Active voice

When a sentence is written in the active voice, the following rule is applied:

> The thing doing the action is the subject.
>
> The thing receiving the action is the object.

For example:

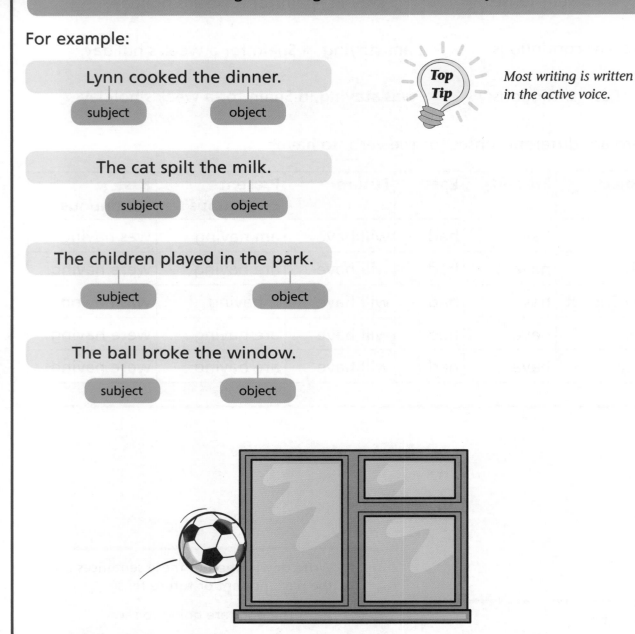

Lynn cooked the dinner.

subject — object

The cat spilt the milk.

subject — object

The children played in the park.

subject — object

The ball broke the window.

subject — object

Top Tip *Most writing is written in the active voice.*

Passive voice

When a sentence is written in the **passive voice**, the following rule is applied:

> The thing receiving the action is the subject.
>
> The thing doing the action can be included but does not have to be.

For example:

The dinner was cooked (by Lynn).

- subject
- object

The milk was spilt (by the cat).

- subject
- object

The park was played in (by the children).

- subject
- object

The window was broken (by a ball).

- subject
- object

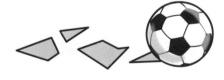

You need a clear understanding of the difference between active and passive voice so that you can control it in your writing.

Top Tip

Key words

active voice

passive voice

Quick test

Write down whether these sentences are in the active or passive form.

1. The race was won by the girl.
2. The box was dropped by the man.
3. James tripped over the stone.
4. The lady stopped the traffic.
5. The jar was passed by George.
6. Cody swam across the pool.

Precision in vocabulary

Standard English in speech

Standard English is when all the rules of English are applied correctly, both in written and verbal communication. There can be some distinction between spoken and written communication but, as a general rule, Standard English should always be applied in formal situations.

A conversation with your friends is likely to contain non-standard English terms as well as **slang** terms and **colloquialisms**.

The friends understand what each other means and they use abbreviations, slang terms and a much more informal manner.

On the other hand, a conversation with a teacher or new acquaintance, or a speech to a group of people, requires a much more formal tone and the use of Standard English.

Standard English in writing

Similar rules apply in writing (as they do in speech) in that the audience and purpose of writing determines the degree to which Standard English is applied. However, the informal use of English must only be used when it is controlled by the writer.

For example, it is acceptable to use slang terms and informal English in an email to a friend, or in a story where two teenagers are talking to each other and the direct speech is shown (as you are developing the characters). However, it is not acceptable to use slang terms and informal writing in a report about a school visit or an autobiography.

Therefore, think: **task**, **audience** and **purpose**. It is important to know what you are writing about before you know the audience.

These factors determine the level of formality in writing.

Writing concisely

Why use 20 words when you can say it in 10? Often writers can fall into the trap of writing long sentences to make their work sound grand! However, this means that the writing can waffle and become boring for the reader, or even incomprehensible. Take care to only use words and sentences that are necessary and get straight to the point.

For example, look at the following two sentences:

> What I meant to say, after thinking about all of the evidence, and my own opinions, is that I agree that school uniform should be worn, although some people won't agree with me.

> Although not everyone will agree, I think school uniform should be worn.

Key words

Standard English

slang

colloquialisms

Quick test

Rewrite these sentences into standard English.

1. I had a wicked time last night with my mates.

2. I ain't gonna bother working hard anymore.

3. I know I shouldn't of done it.

Test practice questions

1 The sentences below each have an error. The errors are underlined. Write the correction in the box to make the subjects and verbs agree.

a) The birds <u>is</u> flying across the sky.

b) Daisy <u>runned</u> quickly to school.

c) Chris and Tim <u>was</u> playing a board game.

1 mark

2 Write this sentence in Standard English.

I love playing with me mates down the park.

_____

1 mark

3 Liam said the grammar <u>lesson</u> was <u>boring</u> but <u>Matilda</u> said she was excited by the end!

Put a tick in each row to show whether each underlined word is a noun or an adjective.

Word from the sentence	Noun	Adjective
lesson		
boring		
Matilda		

1 mark

4 Underline the **four** pronouns in the sentence below.

Maxwell wanted a dog; he had always longed for a dog but his parents would not allow him to have one.

2 marks

5 Draw lines to match each word with the type of word that it is in this sentence.

The man <u>skipped</u> <u>merrily</u> down the <u>road</u>.

skipped		noun
merrily		verb
road		adverb

1 mark

1 Circle the prepositions in this sentence.

The children ran up the hill and then they jumped over the fence!

1 mark

2 Put a tick in each row to show whether the **main** clause or the **subordinate** clause is in bold.

	Main clause	Subordinate clause
My mum, who looks after me very well, **always nags me to tidy my room**.		
The police came to the house because the owners phoned them.		
The computer, **which is brand new**, has stopped working!		

1 mark

3 Put one letter in each box to show the **type of adjective**.

Superlative A	Comparative B	Adjective C

The biggest elephant at the noisy zoo was shorter than the tallest giraffe.

☐   ☐   ☐   ☐

1 mark

4 Circle the **connective** in the sentence below.

Despite the bad weather, the show had to go on!

1 mark

5 Circle the verb in the following sentence:

The loudest dog was the prettiest.

1 mark

Test practice questions

1 Which sentence uses articles correctly?

Tick **one**

A man put the umbrella up as a rain started to fall.

The man put an umbrella up as the rain started to fall.

A man put a umbrella up as the rain started to fall.

The man put a umbrella up as the rain started to fall.

1 mark

2 Underline the **main clause** in the sentence below.

Although there was fire damage, the school was open to children.

1 mark

3 Tick **one** word to complete the sentence below.

The rain was flooding in _____ the roof having been mended!

finally

because

despite

otherwise

1 mark

4 Put one letter in each box to show the **type of connective used in each sentence**.

Coordinating	Subordinating
A	B

a) The elephants were noisy because they were hungry.

b) The rain was pouring down but they still played outside.

c) Freya likes spaghetti and Matilda likes tagliatelli.

2 marks

1 The sentence below is written in the **active** voice.

The headteacher wrote the letter to parents.

Which sentence is the passive form of the sentence above?

Tick **one**

The letter to parents was written by the headteacher. ☐

The parents asked the headteacher to write the letter. ☐

The letter, written by the headteacher, was sent to parents. ☐

The headteacher wrote to the parents, in a letter. ☐   **1 mark**

2 Put a tick in each row to show the type of adverb.

	Adverb of time	Adverb of place	Adverb of manner	Adverb of frequency
yesterday				
occasionally				
quietly				
inside				

1 mark

3 Rewrite the sentence below, changing the verbs to the **past** tense.

The children are playing happily in the park and then they are going home.

_____   **1 mark**

4 Put one letter in each box to show the **type of noun**.

Abstract AB	Collective CL	Common CM	Proper PR

Isaac watched the flock of birds fly across the beautiful sky with curiosity.

☐   ☐   ☐   ☐   **1 mark**

5 Circle the correct form of the verb in each set of brackets.

Shirley and Jo (has / have) the same job.

Everyone (is / are) allowed to stand on their seats.

The children (work / works) hard to learn their grammar.   **1 mark**

Full stops, capital letters and more

Full stops and capital letters

Punctuation ensures that writing makes sense. Without any punctuation, the words would just be altogether in a passage. **Full stops** and **capital letters** are the most basic forms of punctuation, and without them, we would not understand what the text means.

Look at this passage:

> The children went for a walk in the sunny park they played on the swings and the roundabout sadly it then started to rain so they had to go home

The text does not make much sense and it is very hard to read. Now look at the same passage with full stops and capital letters:

> The children went for a walk in the sunny park. They played on the swings and the roundabout. Sadly, it then started to rain so they had to go home.

This makes much more sense and is easier to read.

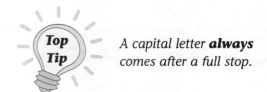

*A capital letter **always** comes after a full stop.*

Proper nouns

Proper nouns are names for individual people, places, events or organisations. They always begin with a capital letter, even if they are in the middle of a sentence. They are the only words that have capital letters in the middle of sentences.

> I am meeting with Sharon when I travel to France at the beginning of February.

The proper nouns in this example are Sharon, France and February.

The pronoun 'I' is always written as a capital, never as a lower case i.

In English, the days of the week and months of the year are seen as proper nouns.

Question marks

Question marks are used at the end of words or sentences to indicate a direct question.

Hello, how are you feeling today?

Not very well, I fell out of a tree yesterday. How are you?

Exclamation marks

Exclamation marks are used at the end of words or sentences when the writer wants to indicate a strong feeling, such as surprise, anger or joy. They are often used to show when someone is speaking loudly or shouting.

Help! Help!

Stop thief!

Top Tip

*Exclamation marks and question marks are used **instead** of full stops in sentences that are exclaimed or are questions, **never in addition** to. Capital letters always start the new sentence after the punctuation.*

Key words

full stop
capital letter
question mark
exclamation mark

Quick test

Write the correct punctuation to finish these sentences.

1. How much longer is this journey going to be

2. Fire

3. I had ham, peas and chips for tea last night

4. I have 2 sisters

5. Goodness gracious

Commas, colons & semi-colons

Commas in lists

Commas are used to separate items in a list when the items are individual or two-word items.

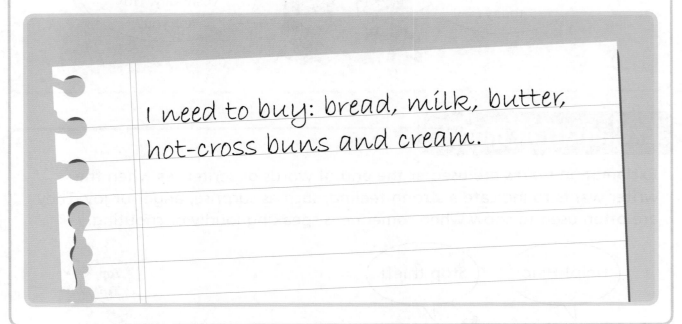

I need to buy: bread, milk, butter, hot-cross buns and cream.

Commas in sentences

Commas are used to mark a brief pause to help make the meaning of a sentence clearer. They can be used to separate main **clauses** from subordinate clauses in **complex sentences** (see pages 16–17).

Look at this sentence without a comma:

The boy turned to his mum and said: "Let's eat mum."

Now look at the same sentence with a comma:

The boy turned to his mum and said: "Let's eat, mum."

In the first sentence it sounds like the boy is going to eat his mum! In the second sentence, the comma makes it clear that they will eat a meal together.

Top Tip

Check your sentences carefully to make sure you have not left out any important commas.

Colons

Colons are used to signal that something is going to follow that is important, e.g. the start of a list or an explanation. Colons are also used in play scripts to show a character's lines.

> **Juliet**: O Romeo, Romeo, wherefore art thou Romeo?...

> **Romeo**: [Aside] Shall I hear more, or shall I speak at this?

Semi-colons

Level 6

Semi-colons can be used in two ways:

1. To replace a full stop (as it links two complete sentences that are closely related, making them into one).

> The rain was pouring from the sky; I couldn't go out and play football.

2. To separate items in a list if using commas would be confusing (when items are longer than one or two words).

> I need to pack: a sleeping bag for night-time; a compass to find the way; a tent to sleep in and a torch to light the way.

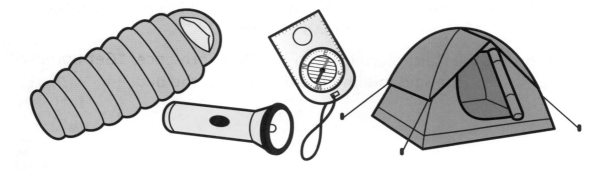

Key words

comma

clause

complex sentence

colon

semi-colon

Quick test

Add commas to these sentences to help them make sense.

1. The teacher said we needed: pens pencils rubbers and crayons.

2. Despite the sunshine the ground was still wet.

3. Mary who was very fit ran in the London marathon.

Inverted commas

What are inverted commas?

Inverted commas are also called speech marks or quotation marks. They are used to show the exact words that someone has spoken. This is also called **direct speech**.

> The teacher said, "Use inverted commas properly!"

*Whenever a person **starts** speaking, the sentence begins with a capital letter after the opening of the inverted comma.*

Direct speech

Direct speech is used to show the words that a person has actually spoken. A new line is started for each new speaker. The words **outside** the inverted commas show **who** is speaking, whilst the words **inside** the inverted commas show exactly **what** has been spoken.

> "Wake up! Wake up!" shouted Mum from downstairs.
>
> "Just five more minutes," Jason replied, pulling the duvet up around his ears.
>
> Footsteps on the stairs alerted Jason to Mum's presence, "Get up now!" she said, pulling the duvet from the bed.

*When you finish a sentence, the full stop or punctuation mark **must** be inside the final inverted comma, e.g. "Help!"*

Reported speech

Reported speech is when the reader is told about something that has been said. Inverted commas are not used in reported speech as it is not showing the actual words that are spoken.

Reported speech:

> The man was calling for help loudly as he hung on by one finger to the cliff edge. His echo was the only thing that he heard, repeating his words back to him.

As direct speech this would be:

> "Help! Help!" shouted the man loudly as he hung on by one finger to the cliff edge.
>
> "Help! Help!" his echo replied.

To help you change sentences from direct speech into reported speech, try starting the sentence with the subject of the sentence, and be prepared to add, delete or change some words. For example:

Direct speech: "Will you come to the cinema with me?" Shirley asked her brother.

Reported speech: **Shirley** *asked her brother* **if he would go** *to the cinema with her.*

Quick test

Change these sentences into reported speech.

1. "Can you help me?" the man asked, "I need to buy some chocolate."

2. The lady walked into the kitchen and screamed, "What a mess!"

3. "I need you to think more carefully," said the policeman, to the suspect, "about where you were last night."

4. "I am so excited about the weekend," Sophie exclaimed, "because I am competing in a swimming gala!"

5. "Where are we going today Dad?" asked Mary.

Key words

inverted commas

direct speech

reported speech

Apostrophes

What are apostrophes?

Apostrophes are punctuation marks that look like single speech marks. They are used in two ways:

1. To show **omission** of letters (**contraction**).

2. To indicate **possession**.

Apostrophes for contraction or omission

Apostrophes for contraction are used for words where a letter or letters have been removed (omitted). This can be referred to as either **contraction** or **omission** and it is important that you remember both of these terms.

Words that have been contracted are used in informal writing, but they are never used in formal writing when Standard English is required.

Here are some examples of common contractions:

I cannot	=	I can't
I am	=	I'm
we have	=	we've
does not	=	doesn't
she will	=	she'll
you are	=	you're
did not	=	didn't
they are	=	they're
who is	=	who's
should not	=	shouldn't
should have	=	should've

Apostrophes for contraction / omission can be used in writing where the audience and purpose dictate that it can be informal, e.g. a letter to a friend, or direct speech in a story.

Make sure you put the apostrophe where the letters have been omitted, for example: shouldn't – the apostrophe shows that the letter 'o' has been omitted.

Apostrophes for possession

Apostrophes for possession are used to show that something belongs to somebody. In the simplest rule, you add an apostrophe followed by an 's' if the word does not end in an 's' already.

The dress that belongs to the woman = the woman's dress

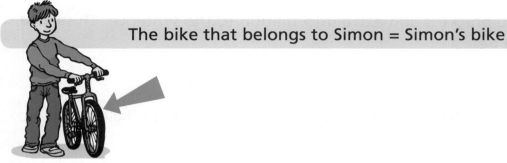

The bike that belongs to Simon = Simon's bike

If the word already ends in an 's' and is a singular subject, then you add an apostrophe and a second 's':

The house belonging to Chris = Chris's house

If the word already ends in an 's' and is a plural subject, then you add an apostrophe after the word and do **not** add another 's':

The car belonging to the Smiths = The Smiths' car.

Top Tip

*The word **it's** only ever has an apostrophe to show contraction / omission for the words 'it is' or 'it has'. It **never** has an apostrophe to mark possession.*

Quick test

Write whether the apostrophe is being used for possession or omission / contraction.

1. I shan't have time to buy everything!
2. James's toys were all neatly packed away.
3. It's not fair that I can't have a horse!
4. He'll be along shortly.
5. It was too late to stop the Jones' car being stolen.

Key words

apostrophe

omission

contraction

possession

Brackets and dashes

What are brackets?

Brackets are used in pairs around a group of words that need to be kept separate within a sentence.

The words in the brackets add extra information to the sentence. This extra information can be:

- an interruption

  > I knew he was cheating (I was not wrong) which is why I challenged him.

- an explanation:

  > The children (who were all in class 6) were at school early
  > for their visit to London.

- an afterthought:

  > I watched the car closely (which was going too fast, in my opinion)
  > to try and remember the number plate.

What is a dash?

A dash is double the size of a hyphen and is a horizontal line that marks pauses within sentences. There are two ways that dashes can be used:

1. **Double dashes**, e.g. He was angry – and rightly so – because he had his wallet stolen.

2. A **single dash**, e.g. I waited patiently – and it was almost too much to bear.

Double dashes

Double dashes are used in a similar way to brackets as they separate groups of words from the rest of the sentence. This only occurs when the group of words comes in the middle of a sentence. They mark a less strong division than brackets.

> The machinery – two JCBs, three cranes and two steamrollers – was brought to the building.

To demonstrate your abilities as a writer, it is important to display a range of punctuation throughout your writing. Dashes are a great alternative to brackets.

Top Tip

Single dash

A single dash is used to mark an expectant pause in a sentence:

> He looked into the darkness – two yellow eyes stared back.

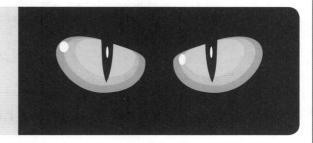

They can also be used before a change of direction in a sentence:

> The children all lined up outside – it was time for the spelling test.

Quick test

Add brackets or dashes to these sentences to make them more understandable for the reader.

1 The man was staring thoughtfully at the house I didn't know him.

2 Buckingham Palace where the Queen lives is in London.

3 The new houses six bungalows and two blocks of flats were opened this morning.

4 The man crept through the door he came face to face with a bear!

Key words

brackets

double dashes

single dash

Hyphens and ellipsis

What is a hyphen?

A **hyphen** is only half the length of a dash. It is used between words to create a linking mark to make a new word or expression.

For example:

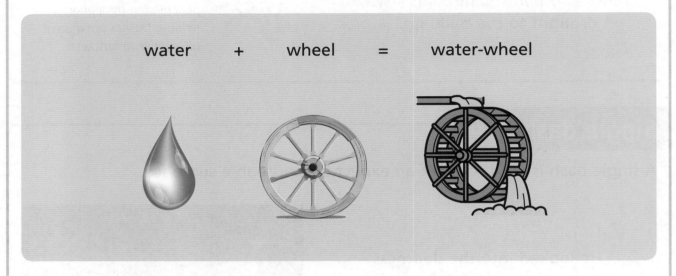

water + wheel = water-wheel

red + hot = red-hot

twelve + year + old = twelve-year-old

What is an ellipsis?

An **ellipsis** is a punctuation mark used in different ways to add meaning to sentences. It can be used in the following ways:

- To shorten quotations
- To leave sentences for the reader to fill in details
- To build suspense
- To indicate interruption

Ellipsis for suspense or filling in gaps

To show suspense, you can leave sentences unfinished at the end of a chapter, and allow the reader to fill in the gaps.

> They peered into the dark room and saw…

You can also leave a sentence unfinished at the end of a story if you want to leave your reader to fill in their own idea.

> In the distance, there was the sound of an engine…

Ellipsis for interruptions

Ellipses are also used to show that one sentence has interrupted another, particularly when using direct speech in writing.

"Do I have to…" Jane whined.

"Tidy your room? Yes you do!" snapped Mum

"But…" Jane continued.

"No buts," replied Mum in an exasperated voice, "just get on with it!"

Key words

hyphen

ellipsis

Quick test

Add a hyphen and a word to make new words or phrases.

1. ice
2. twenty
3. mid
4. spot

Full use of punctuation

Why use punctuation?

Punctuation allows readers to make sense of the meaning of sentences, paragraphs and whole texts. Without punctuation it would be nearly impossible to understand texts.

For example, look at the text below:

> I woke up one morning and remembered the dream that I had had when I had been lying in my bed I think I must have woken up because I was scared when the dragon was chasing me not a real dragon the dragon in my dream you understand I know that in my dream I chased the dragon away using the sword that I had been given but I woke up so I still dont know what happened to the dragon in the end I certainly dont want another dream like that one.

Whilst you are able to get the gist of the account, it is not easy to gain real meaning from it as there are no places to pause. Now look at this text:

> I woke up one morning and remembered the dream that I had had (when I had been lying in my bed). I think I must have woken up because I was scared when the dragon was chasing me (not a real dragon; the dragon in my dream, you understand). I know that in my dream I chased the dragon away, using the sword that I had been given, but I woke up, so I still don't know what happened to the dragon in the end! I certainly don't want another dream like that one...

Whilst this writing still needs editing in terms of sentence structure and vocabulary choices, the second example conveys a great deal more understanding to the reader than the first example.

Types of punctuation

As a Level 6 writer, you are expected to be able to use the full range of **punctuation** marks throughout your writing. This does not mean that in every single piece of writing you need all of the types of punctuation, but it does mean that across a range of your writing you need to show that you can use them all.

,   commas to indicate a brief pause

...   ellipsis for suspense / quote shortening

" "   inverted commas for direct speech

;   semi-colons to link two related sentences

:   colons to indicate the start of a list, quote or explanation

( )   brackets to separate parts of a sentence

—   dashes to separate parts of a sentence

-   hyphens to link two words to create a new word

'   apostrophes used for contraction (omission) and possession

Key words

punctuation	colon
comma	brackets
ellipsis	dash
inverted commas	hyphen
semi-colon	apostrophe

Quick test

Write your own short description about a place you know well, making sure that you use at least 6 **different** types of punctuation in your writing.

Test practice questions

1 Write these sentences using the correct punctuation.

it is going to be my birthday in may i am going to invite all of my friends to my party

_____

_____ **1 mark**

2 Draw lines to show the correct punctuation to end each of these sentences.

| How many times have you been to France | | ? |

| Wow, that's amazing | | . |

| I have green eyes | | ! | **1 mark**

3 Write a question starting with the word 'Where'.

Where _____ **1 mark**

4 Which sentence uses commas correctly?

Tick one

I had to pack: shirts, trousers, socks and pants. ☐

I had to pack, shirts, trousers, socks and pants. ☐

I had to pack, shirts. trousers. socks and pants. ☐

I had to pack: shirts trousers, socks and pants. ☐ **1 mark**

1 Which of the sentences below uses **commas** correctly?

Tick **one**

The man, stopped looked intently at the floor, then hurried on. ☐

The man stopped, looked intently, at the floor then hurried on. ☐

The man stopped, looked intently at the floor, then hurried on. ☐

The man stopped looked intently at the floor, then hurried on. ☐   **1 mark**

2 Insert **three** commas in the correct places in the sentence below.

I have to take a rucksack a sleeping bag a torch biscuits and a warm hat

1 mark

3 Write Matthew's words as direct speech.

Matthew said that he was going on holiday to Spain in the summer.

_____

_____ **1 mark**

4 Put a tick to show whether the apostrophe in each sentence is used for **omission** or **possession**.

	Apostrophe for omission	Apostrophe for possession
It's still raining outside.		
They're all waiting for the bus!		
It was Max's turn next.		

1 mark

Test practice questions

1 Look at this sentence:

The children (who were away from their parents at camp) were working on their teambuilding skills.

a) What is the name of the punctuation mark that is used after the words 'children' and 'camp'?

_____

b) Why is this punctuation mark used in the sentence above?

Tick **one** box.

To show that there is a list coming up ☐

To add additional information ☐

To add an afterthought ☐

To show that someone is speaking ☐   **1 mark**

2 Tick one box to show where an ellipsis would be added to the sentence below to add a pause for tension.

The TV presenter announced that the winner was Bob the Builder!   **1 mark**

3 Which sentence uses brackets correctly?

Tick **one** box.

Tower Bridge which was built between (1886 and 1894) spans the River Thames. ☐

Tower Bridge which was built between 1886 and 1894 (spans the River Thames). ☐

(Tower Bridge which was built between 1886 and 1894) spans the River Thames. ☐

Tower Bridge (which was built between 1886 and 1894) spans the River Thames. ☐

1 mark

1 Insert a **colon** in the appropriate place in the sentence below.

I need to buy bread (wholemeal), milk (semi-skimmed) and butter.   **1 mark**

2 A semi-colon can be used to separate two main clauses that are related to each other. Insert a semi-colon in the correct place in the sentence below.

The sun is shining brightly in the sky I will invite my friends for a barbecue.   **1 mark**

3 Match the contraction to the correct words below.

we have		we'd
we will		we'll
we did		we've

1 mark

4 Write this **direct speech** as **reported speech**.

"I won't be able to visit you this weekend," David said to his mother, "as I am going to a concert."

_____

_____   **1 mark**

5 Circle the word that contains the apostrophe that has been used to show possession.

We'll have to go and own up that we damaged Scott's car.   **1 mark**

Prefixes and suffixes

What is a prefix?

A **prefix** is a group of letters that can be added to the front of other words to change their meaning. There are many common prefixes which you will already be familiar with, even if you have not identified them as a prefix.

tri- + -cycle = tricycle

pro- + -test = protest

ab- + -normal = abnormal

Top Tip

If you can learn the meaning and spelling of common prefixes this will help both your spelling and understanding of vocabulary for your writing.

What is a suffix?

A **suffix** is a group of letters that is added to the end of a word to change the way that you use it. A suffix can often change the type of word to a different type, e.g. adjective to verb.

> ship- (*noun / verb*) + -ed = shipped (*verb*)

> hope (*abstract noun*) + -ing = hoping (*verb*)

> clean (*adjective / adverb or noun*) + -er = cleaner (*noun / adjective*)

In these examples, different suffixes have been added and in some cases the final **consonant** has been doubled before the suffix is added.

As a general rule, the final consonant is doubled if the preceding vowel would otherwise change from short to long. For example, 'shop' becomes shopping rather than shoping where it would sound similar to 'hoping'. This is not always the case, but can be used as a general rule.

Another helpful rule to remember is: if a word ends with an e, the e is removed before the suffix is added (if the suffix starts with a **vowel**).

> hope = hoping / hoped

> wake = waking

> gate = gated

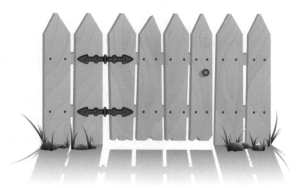

Quick test

For each of the root words below...
- Add a prefix to the root word to make a new word.
- Add a suffix to the root word to make a new word.

1 nourish

2 lead

3 take

4 active

More complex prefixes & suffixes

What are more complex prefixes and suffixes?

More complex **prefixes** and **suffixes** are ones that are not used as regularly as the more common ones (see pages 50–51). To demonstrate your higher levels of understanding, it is important that you use (and control your use of) a range of wider range of vocabulary, incorporating more complex prefixes and suffixes.

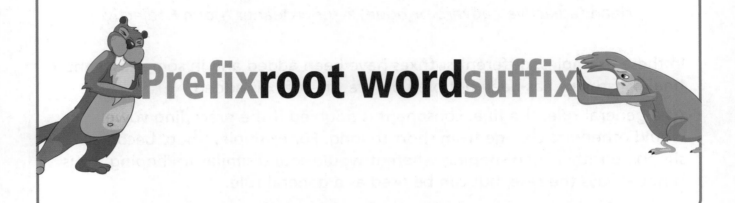

More prefixes

The following are the complex prefixes that you should know. Look at them carefully and become familiar with their meanings.

Prefix	Meaning	Example
agri-	pertaining to fields / soil	agriculture
ali-	other	alias
ap-	away from, detached	apocalypse
bio-	life	biology
chron-	time	chronology
il-	not	illegal
ir-	not	irresponsible
re-	back, again	report
syn-	together, at the same time	syndicate
trans-	across, beyond, change	transform
un-	not, against, opposite	unequal

More suffixes

The following are the complex suffixes that you should know. Look at them carefully and become familiar with their meanings.

Suffix	Meaning	Example
-able	worth, ability (adjective)	workable
-ible	worth, ability (adjective)	incredible
-age	activity (noun)	courage
-ess	female	goddess
-iatry	art of healing	psychiatry
-ify	cause (verb)	intensify
-ory	place for (noun)	territory
-ward	in a direction of manner (adverb)	onward
-wise	with regard to (adverb)	otherwise

Top Tip

By learning the meaning of prefixes and suffixes, you can use this knowledge to work out what longer, more complex words might mean when you come across them in your reading.

Quick test

Write down the meaning of the prefix / suffix in these words, using the charts above and opposite to help you. You could then use a dictionary to find out exactly what each word means and compare that to the meaning of the suffixes / prefixes.

1 podiatry

2 illiterate

3 forward

4 alibi

Key words

prefix

suffix

Vowels and consonants

What are vowels?

The five **vowels** in the English language are:

a e i o u

Some interesting facts about vowels:

- The most common vowel (and letter) in English is 'e'.
- The second most common vowel is 'a'.
- Every syllable in English must have a vowel sound (these can sometimes be the letters 'y' or 'w' functioning as a second vowel).

Vowel sounds

Every syllable in the English language contains a vowel sound. Have a look at these examples:

a-gain (vowel sounds: 'a' and 'ai')

be-cause (vowel sounds: 'ee' and 'au')

hope-ful-ly (vowel sounds: 'o', 'uh' and 'ee')

What are consonants?

There are 21 **consonants** in the English language and they are all the letters that are not vowels.

b c d f g h j k l m n p q r s t v w x y z

Consonant sounds

A consonant letter usually represents one consonant sound. However, some consonant letters (c, g, s) can represent two or more different sounds.

For example:

The letter 'c' can make the following sounds:

k	cake
q	cue
s	notice
sh	special
x	access

The letter 'g' can make the following sounds:

g	global
j	suggest
zh	rouge

Quick test

Write down words where the consonant makes the following sound.

1. h
2. s
3. d
4. k

Homophones and homonyms

What are homophones?

Homophones are words that sound the same as each other but are spelt differently. They can cause confusion in speech as you cannot see the spelling that is being applied. So, you need to use the context of the sentence to help you understand the meaning of a homophone.

The homophones in the table below are all words that are in regular use. In your writing, you must make sure that you use the correct spelling to avoid confusion for your reader.

poor	paw	pour
there	their	they're
break	brake	
grate	great	
hare	hair	
where	wear	
two	too	
blue	blew	

What are homonyms?

Homonyms are words that have the same spelling but different meanings. These can cause further confusion in speech / written text, as it is up to the reader / listener to interpret which of the meanings needs to be applied to the context.

For example, look at the sentence below:

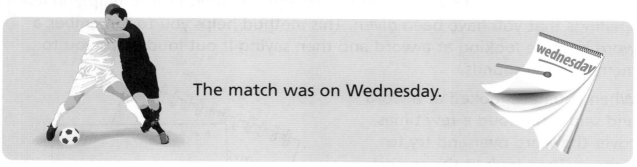

The match was on Wednesday.

There are two possible interpretations of the sentence above (as you can see from the pictures). The reader / listener has to think, within the context of the writing or conversation, which is most likely – in this case it is unlikely somebody would be telling you that a matchstick is lying on the word Wednesday.

Here are some more common examples of homonyms.

bank	light	sink	park

Quick test

Write a definition for each part of the following homophones.

1 sale, sail

2 beach, beech

3 wait, weight

4 key, quay

5 tale, tail

Spelling strategies 1

Look/Say/Cover/Write/Check

The 'look / say / cover / write / check' strategy is a good way to help you learn **spellings** that you have been given. This method helps you to remember a word because looking at a word and then saying it out loud helps you to memorise the sounds.

When you have looked at a word and said it out loud a few times, cover the word over and try to write it. Then look at the correct spelling to see if you are right. If you are, be pleased and then keep rehearsing it daily so that it moves to your long-term memory. If you have made an error, spend more time looking at and saying the word before having another go.

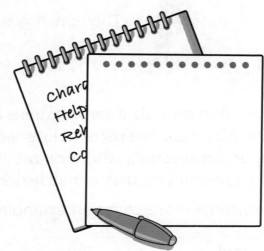

Words within words

Another good strategy for helping you learn longer, more difficult words, is to look for words within words. If you can spot shorter words (that you are already able to spell) it can help you to break a longer word down into smaller parts. This can give you more confidence with spelling a difficult word.

For example: character

Within this word is the word 'act' which is quite easy to remember because when you play a character you are putting on an 'act'. So, by pulling out the shorter word, you can then learn the beginning and end so that it does not become so daunting to learn the whole word in one go.

You can also break a word into **syllables** to help you remember each part. By saying each of the syllables out loud, you will begin to memorise each part and think about the spellings.

For example: help-ful-ly   i-den-ti-cal   in-ter-pre-ta-tion

Air writing

Air writing can be an effective method of learning your spellings, especially if you like to move about when learning, rather than sitting in one place and concentrating for long periods.

Pretend your finger is a large whiteboard marker and write the words that you have been given to learn (spelling lists, corrections...) in the air in big writing. It is up to you what colour, font, size to write in as only you can see it.

Exciting writing

After rehearsing your spellings using your air writing, use bright colours to write the words on a piece of paper in fun ways so that your brain can recall them when you no longer have the piece of paper in front of you.

Top Tip

This is a really useful way of helping your brain memorise a word, as you are seeing it differently from just a list in black writing on white paper.

Key words

spelling

syllable

Quick test

Choose ten words (your current spellings or words that you often spell wrong) and write down all ten words. Check the correct spellings and then write down your score. Now use all or some of the methods above to help you learn them. Re-test yourself and see if your score has improved.

Spelling strategies 2

Saying it as it is spelt

When words have hidden letters in them, it can help with your spelling to pronounce (say) them in funny ways, i.e. breaking them down into syllables but pronouncing the hidden letters clearly.

A good example is **business**. When you pronounce this word it sounds like **biz-ness**, which does not sound the same as the spelling. But, if you pronounce it in a silly way like **bus-i-ness**, you can easily remember each part for spelling.

Mnemonics

Mnemonics are a fun way to learn spellings. You assign a word to each letter of a word so that it makes a memorable phrase. The sillier or funnier the better, as you are more likely to picture / remember it. Try to choose words that give you strong images in your head.

please: **P**irates **L**eave **E**normous **A**nchors **S**ubmerged **E**verywhere

grammar: **G**randma **R**an **A**round **M**ickey **M**ouse **A**nd **R**udolph

Top Tip

The words in the phrase need to create a picture in your head so you need to choose wacky and silly ideas to make this a good strategy.

Rapping

Rapping can be a fun way to learn spellings, especially if you find that you learn better when you hear things being spoken / sung.

Each chant / rap can be different, so you just need to say the letters of each word in a rhythmic way so that it creates a sound you can remember. Try it, it's fun!

Drawing pictures

Drawing a picture can help you to remember a word. This does not mean drawing a picture of the meaning of the word, it means that, for some words, you can write the word itself in the shape of what it is.

Black list

You should be aware of the spellings that you often make mistakes with. These might already be recorded in your spelling journals. Make sure you add to these and use the strategies on the last few pages to help you learn them so that they can come off the black list.

When you struggle with a word, don't bury your head and think you will never be able to spell it. Try different strategies and you will find one that works for that particular word.

Key words

spelling

mnemonics

Quick test

Go through your work and create a 'black list' of words that you commonly spell incorrectly. Use the strategies on the last four pages to help you learn these and be proud when you can take them off your black list when you have learned them.

Word families, roots and origins

Root words

In the English language, many words are derived from other words. The original words are called 'root words'. When you are learning to spell complex words it can be helpful to look for hidden roots (which you have probably already learned to spell in other words).

For example, the root word '**multi**' is contained in the following words: **multicoloured, multimedia** and **multitasking**. The meaning of this root word is: many or more than one of. It can be helpful to know the meaning of the root words as this also helps you know what longer words mean.

Top Tip

Learn the meaning and spelling of the most common root words and then you will be able to apply these to a whole range of words in the English language.

Word origins

Many of the root words that we use today originate from Latin and Greek. Every root word has a meaning and that meaning corresponds to the new word made from it.

The word '**aqua**' comes from the Latin word for 'water'.

Aqua means **water**.

Aquatic means (as an adjective) of, or relating to water.

Word families

Groups of words that come from (or derive from) the same root words are called 'word families'.

aqua → Some of the words in this word family are:

aquatic

aquarium

aqueduct

aquamarine

aqualung

multi → Some of the words in this word family are:

multimedia

multilingual

multimillionaire

multiple

multiply

Key words

root word

origin

word family

Quick test

Find out the meaning of the following root words:

1. art
2. counter
3. inter
4. poly
5. trans

More complex word families

Types of word families

Word families are groups of words that are linked by having a common **root word** (see p. 63). Word families can further be divided into two types of families:

- **form-based** families

- **meaning-based** families.

Form-based families

Form-based families are when a word family is formed from words that have common root words or letter strings in them, i.e. you can see a similarity between the way that they are written through the letters that they contain.

Examples:

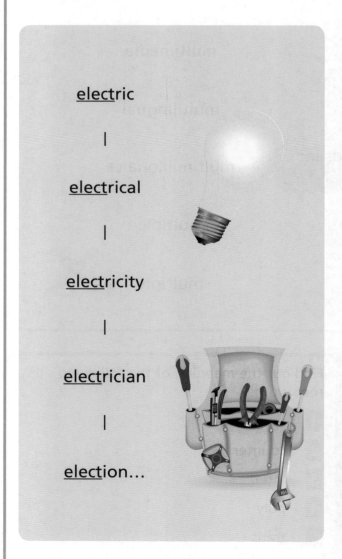

electric

|

electrical

|

electricity

|

electrician

|

election...

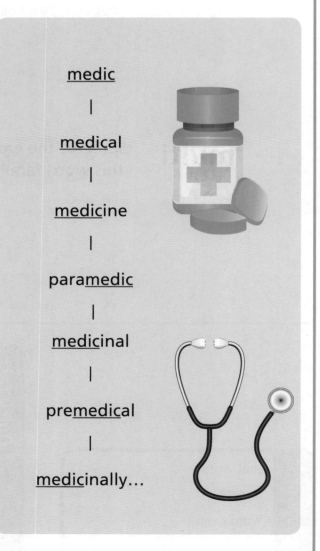

medic

|

medical

|

medicine

|

paramedic

|

medicinal

|

premedical

|

medicinally...

Meaning-based families

Meaning-based families are when a word family is formed from words that relate in meaning but not in form.

They do not contain a common root or letter string and do not look the same when they are written.

Examples:

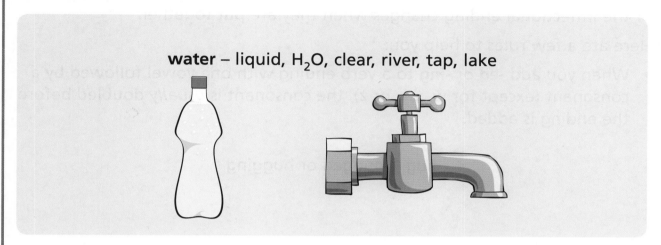

water – liquid, H_2O, clear, river, tap, lake

kitchen – cooking, food, cutlery, crockery, saucepan, utensil

Quick test

Write 5 words that would fit into a meaning-based word family for the following words.

1 window

2 desk

3 computer

4 mirror

Inflectional endings

What is an inflectional ending?

Inflectional endings are common letter strings that are added at the end of a root word, very much like suffixes. Sometimes the spelling of the root word or the inflectional ending changes when they are put together.

Here are a few rules to help you:

- When you add **-ed** or **-ing** to a verb ending with one vowel followed by a consonant (except for w, x, y or z), the consonant is *usually* doubled before the ending is added.

> hug = hugged or hugging

> shrug = shrugged or shrugging

> skip = skipped or skipping

> pedal = pedalled or pedalling

- When you add **-ed** or **-ing** to a verb ending with a consonant and then an 'e', the 'e' is dropped before the ending is added.

> make + ing = making

> name + ed = named

What is an inflectional ending?

- When you add **-ed** or **-es** to a verb ending with a 'y' with a consonant before it, the 'y' is replaced with an 'i' before adding the 'ed' or 'es' ending.

> marry + ed = married

> carry + es = carries

- When you add **-ed** or **-es** to a verb ending in a 'y' with a vowel before it, simply add 'ed' or 'es'.

> play + ed = played

> enjoy + ing = enjoying

Quick test

Add the inflectional ending 'ed' to these words, remembering the spelling rules needed.

1 meddle
2 tug
3 hurry
4 look
5 grin

Editing skills

What is editing and why do we do it?

Editing is a very important part of any writing process as it helps to make sure that your writing is as close to perfect as possible, without spelling and grammatical errors. It can be quite easy, when writing, to be thinking so quickly and to become so involved in the creative process or the action of the story, that mistakes can be made in the writing, e.g. like spelling words incorrectly or forgetting to write all of the words in a sentence.

A published book, like this one, will have many checking stages. For example, the text written by the author will be sent to an editor who checks for errors, and then proofreaders and technical readers will check the book at several different stages.

When you produce a piece of writing, it is very important that you check it and read back through it several times, as you have to play the important role of writer and editor. There are several things you need to look out for:

- spelling and punctuation errors
- repetition of words
- making sure your sentences make sense
- will your reader be interested throughout the whole piece of writing?

Spelling and punctuation errors

On your first read through, you need to look out for any spelling errors (especially where you may have used the wrong homophone) and punctuation omissions. You need to check that you have used a range of punctuation and that you have not missed any obvious things (like forgetting to put a question mark at the end of a question).

Repetition and making sense

On your second read through, you need to make sure that you have not used the same word too often. Common words that are overused are connectives and words like 'because', 'nice' and 'said'. Where you find **repetition**, think of alternative words (**synonyms**) and change them by putting a neat line through your original word and writing the new word above. Or take out any sentences that are the same as the previous one.

As you read through your writing, you need to read every sentence slowly and double check that all the words you think are there have, in fact, been written. It is very easy to miss words out when you are writing quickly and your brain, as the author, knows what it is meant to say, so fills in the gaps. Take time to read the text slowly to check for these types of errors.

Think about your reader

On your final read through, you should imagine that you are the reader and think about the enjoyment value of the writing. Will it keep your reader interested throughout? Have you used exciting vocabulary? If not, now is your chance to change some of your words to make them more engaging for your reader.

Key words

editing

repetition

synonyms

Quick test

Edit this piece of writing using the suggestions above.

Emily walked to work slowly and thoughtfully! If only she had a car, she would not have to walk every morning and every knight. Her feet were always sore by the end of the day from all the walking. Her feet hurt her all day and then hurt again in the evening. She was going to bye a car. But wear would she get the money.

Test practice questions

1 The sentences below each have an error. The errors are underlined. Write the correction in the box, choosing the correct homophone.

The socks were matched into their correct <u>pears</u>.

It was <u>they're</u> turn to go on the ride.

It was <u>two</u> difficult to reach a decision.

1 mark

2 Identify the word that is spelt incorrectly and write the correct spelling in the box.

The busness is turning over a huge profit. **1 mark**

3 Write the prefix that can be added to the following words.

-verb

-dress

-verse

_____

1 mark

4 Write two examples of words containing each of the following suffixes:

-ly		
-ed		

1 mark

1 The word **wave** has more than one meaning.

Write two sentences to show two **different** meanings.

a) _____

_____

b) _____

_____ **1 mark**

2 Rewrite this sentence correctly.

The jewellry box lifes on my spesial shelf in my bedroom.

_____

_____ **1 mark**

3 Put a tick in each row to show whether the word has one, two or three syllables.

Word	One syllable	Two syllables	Three syllables
helpful			
hopefully			
fruit			
pencil			

1 mark

4 Add a suffix to create a verb in the past tense.

Help_____ **1 mark**

5 Write three words containing the root word 'aqua'.

_____ _____ _____ **1 mark**

Test practice questions

1 Put a tick in each row to show which inflectional ending rule must be applied to each of the words shown.

	add 'd'	double the final consonant before adding -ed	add -ed
help			
trudge			
shame			
hop			

1 mark

2 A prefix is a letter or group of letters added to the beginning of a word to make a new word.

For example: **mal**nutrition

Put a prefix at the beginning of each word to make it mean the opposite.

_____prove

_____attractive

_____trust

1 mark

3 Find **one** word that can complete **both** sentences below.

Write the word in the box.

She wore a beautiful gold _____ on her finger.

The school asked parents to _____ for an appointment.

1 mark

1 Write three words with the prefix 'un'.

_____

_____

_____ **1 mark**

2 Circle the correct spelling of each of these words.

suiteable / suiteble / suitable

foreign / foriegn / forein **1 mark**

3 Add a suffix to these words to change them from verbs to nouns.

write = _____

create = _____ **1 mark**

4 Underline the root word in the following words.

medicine

biology

astronaut **1 mark**

5 Put a tick in each row to show which prefix could be added to each root word.

	un-	dis-	mal-	im-
-personal				
-necessary				
-advantage				
-nutrition				
-patient				

2 marks

Antonyms and synonyms

What are synonyms

Synonyms are words or phrases that mean the same (or nearly the same) as another word or phrase. Using synonyms can avoid your writing becoming repetitive and therefore boring for your reader.

Look how dull this piece of writing is for the reader:

> The pretty sun shone prettily through the trees creating patches of pretty light on the floor; it looked so pretty. The pretty trees...

Now look at the same paragraph that uses synonyms:

> The magnificent sun shone brightly through the trees creating patches of beautiful light on the floor; it looked magical. The majestic trees...

Which would you rather read? Why?

'She said', 'I said', 'he said'

When writing direct speech, it is very easy to fall into the trap of overusing the word 'said':

> Mum said: 'Shall we go for a walk?"
>
> "I can't be bothered," said Sam.
>
> Maddy said: "I'd like to come, especially if we go past the sweet shop."
>
> "Actually I think I will come," said Sam.

Using a synonym for the word 'said' can make a piece of writing far more interesting:

> Mum asked: 'Shall we go for a walk?"
>
> "I can't be bothered," whined Sam.
>
> Maddy answered: "I'd like to come, especially if we go past the sweet shop."
>
> "Actually I think I will come," said Sam.

Top Tip

Make a list, which you can keep near you when writing, of all the synonyms for 'said' to help make your writing interesting for your reader.

What is an antonym?

An **antonym** is a word that is opposite in meaning to another word.
For example:

	sink	float
	thick	thin
	open	closed
	happy	sad

Quick test

Write the antonyms for these words:

1 open
2 hot
3 big
4 boy
5 push
6 quiet

Speech vocabulary

Types of speech

In writing, there are two types of speech:

- **direct speech**
- **reported speech**

> I thought speech was speech!

> No! You can either use the actual words, or report the words that were used.

Direct speech

Direct speech is used when you want to show exactly what a character or person has said. **Inverted commas** (**speech marks**) are used around the words that **are actually spoken**.

> "I love ice-cream!" announced Claire
>
> "So do I!" agreed Rachel

In the example above, Claire has said: "I love ice-cream". So these are the words that have to be in the inverted commas (speech marks). The words 'announced Claire' are not included as these were not actually spoken.

The words in inverted commas (speech marks) can be interrupted by showing who the speaker is. You need to use other punctuation in the sentence correctly too.

> "Stop reading," said the teacher, "and listen to me."

The sentence: 'Stop reading and listen to me' is what the teacher has said. The extra comma after reading is included to indicate the break in the sentence for the speaker to be introduced.

Top Tip

Make sure you use punctuation within the inverted commas (speech marks) correctly, e.g. "We got lost," he explained.

Reported speech

Reported speech is when the words that have been said are reported within the text. There is no need for inverted commas (speech marks) as the actual words are not actually given.

For example:

> Claire announced that she loved ice-cream and Rachel agreed with her.

The words: 'I love ice-cream' are not written, but the events are reported as if they have been said.

> The teacher told the children to stop reading and listen to her.

The word 'me' from the direct speech changes to 'her' when written as reported speech.

Direct speech:

You must do your grammar revision every night!

Reported speech: The teacher told the children that they must do their grammar revision every night.

Quick test

Write these reported speech examples as direct speech.

1 The teacher said that she was going to retire at the end of the year.

2 The clown joked that his smile had slipped from his face.

3 Nancy remarked that her knowledge of grammar had improved.

4 The lady shouted for help.

5 James asked how much further the journey was going to be in a whiny voice.

Singular and plural

What does singular and plural mean?

When you are writing or talking about something that is on its own, it is in its **singular** form.

> cat

When you are writing or talking about more than one thing, it is called a **plural**. Plurals can often be spotted in texts as they end with an 's'. However, this is not always the case as there are separate rules.

> cat = cats

> hat = hats

> car = cars

> flower = flowers

Words that add 'es' in the plural

If a word ends in ch, sh, s, x or z in its singular form, you have to add 'es' instead of just 's' to make it a plural.

> dress = dresses

> box = boxes

Singular words ending in 'y'

If a word ends in a consonant then a 'y', the 'y' is removed and 'ies' is added to make it plural.

> puppy = puppies

> baby = babies

Top Tip

Always look carefully at the letter before the 'y' to decide what the plural should be.

If a word ends in a vowel then a 'y', then you usually add an 's' to make it plural.

> donkey = donkeys

> boy = boys

> day = days

Singular words ending in 'f'

If a word in its singular form ends with an 'f', the 'f' usually changes to 'ves'. Sometimes it just has an 's' added after the 'f'.

leaf = leaves

thief = thieves

roof = roofs

chief = chiefs

dwarf = dwarfs

cliff = cliffs

Singular words ending in 'o'

If a word in its singular form ends with an 'o', the letters 'es' are often added after the 'o' to make it plural.

tomato = tomatoes

potato = potatoes

Top Tip

There are exceptions to this rule too that you need to learn, e.g. pianos, videos, radios, solos.

Key words

singular

plural

Quick test

Write the plural versions of these words.

1 table

2 lady

3 coat

4 calf

5 cargo

Technical vocabulary

What is technical vocabulary?

Technical vocabulary refers to words that are associated with a particular content area or topic. It is most often found in non-fiction books where detailed descriptions of complex objects, ideas or concepts are explained.

For example:

The water cycle

- evaporation
- condensation
- precipitation

What is a desert?

- arid
- minerals
- environment

Life in Ancient Greece

- Acropolis
- hoplite
- mosaic

The technical vocabulary is often put in bold in these non-fiction books, indicating that the definition of the word can be found in the glossary. This is because the technical vocabulary needs to be used in order for the object, idea or concept to be understood, although the reader is not expected to know what it means when they first read it.

When would I use it?

You are likely to write a range of non-fiction texts (and some fiction texts where you are explaining technical points) which will require the use of technical vocabulary. It is important that you control the use of this and do not shy away from using the more complex terminology (you can always add a glossary at the end).

For example, in this article the technical vocabulary has been circled in red.

Climate Change for Kids
Global Warming

Lots of people have studied the climate all around the world. They agreed several years ago that climate change really was happening. As a result, all countries in the world came together in a big conference at Kyoto in Japan.

Here they began to try and agree what to do about climate change. Lots of promises were made but countries haven't been very good at carrying them out.

Since then, the evidence of change has become stronger and stronger. The special computer 'models' which scientists had used have become more and more accurate. The ice sheets in both the Arctic and the Antarctic are melting, in some cases very fast. Sea levels are rising.

Temperatures are rising, especially in the Arctic and Antarctic. Glaciers on other mountains of the world are melting very fast – especially in the Himalayas.

Animals and plants which like warmer conditions are moving further north and south. Yes, it's happening all right.

The world is hotting up. And I'm sorry to say it's all people's fault.

Write a definition for each of these words that could go in a glossary about Ancient Rome.

1. basilica
2. chariot
3. aqueduct
4. hypocaust
5. senate
6. stylus

Key words

technical vocabulary

glossary

Figurative language

What is figurative language?

Literal language is when the words (or phrases) mean exactly what they say.

Figurative language, on the other hand, refers to words (or phrases) that change or exaggerate the actual meaning of the words. **Similes** and **metaphors** are examples of this. This kind of language is used to enhance descriptions in order to engage the reader's interest.

Top Tip

Try to use a range of different types of figurative language throughout your writing to show that you understand the effects they create on the reader.

Personification

Personification is when a non-human thing is described as having, or using, human qualities.

> The tree danced in the breeze.

> The sea leapt onto the rocks.

You can combine similes and metaphors with personification to enhance the description further.

> The tree was a ballerina, dancing in the breeze.

> The sea is like a base-jumper, leaping onto the rocks.

Alliteration

Alliteration is when the same letter or sound is used at the beginning of words that are adjacent or very closely positioned. It can be used to exaggerate a point or to create a particular sound to add to a description.

> The swirling sea sang sweetly...

> Ten tall towers...

Assonance

Assonance is based on the sounds of the words, like alliteration, but it refers to the repetition of vowel sounds within the words (rather than at the beginning) to create an internal rhyme.

> The goose was loose from the noose!

> I sigh, and cry for the fly!

Onomatopoeia

Onomatopoeia is when a word is formed from the sound that is associated with it. It is a great tool to use if you want to focus or surprise your reader.

Quick test

Which type of figurative language is used in each example?

1. smash
2. The house stood tall.
3. Eight eggs edged along!
4. The maze was a riddle.
5. The cat in the hat was fat.

Personal form and impersonal form

Impersonal language

Impersonal language is used for formal pieces of writing where you are not expressing your own opinion. Here is a brief outline and checklist to use to check that you are writing in an impersonal form:

- It should not contain the personal pronoun 'I'.
- It should not contain personal opinions.
- It should not contain judgemental words.
- It should, if written in the impersonal voice, be in the third person.

The wearing of school uniform is a common occurrence in schools in England. Some children may start wearing a school uniform from as early as the age of three, if they start in a school nursery. There are a variety of different uniform styles and items; some can be formal (blazer, pleated skirts or trousers, white shirts and ties), whilst others can be more informal (sweatshirts and polo shirts). In essence, the uniform shows that one belongs to a particular establishment (in this case a school). The wearing of the uniform can be modified by the pupils, but remains, in some way still affiliated with the dress code for that establishment.

Some people may agree with the wearing of uniforms for pupils as they can foster an ethos of friendship, belonging and hard work. These people may argue that without a uniform each pupil attending the school remains an individual.

On the other hand, some people may argue that by wearing a uniform a pupil simply becomes one small member of a group and therefore loses their identity as an individual. The people that argue this point may also say that the cost of the uniform becomes too great for parents who are unable to afford to replace items when they are worn out or damaged.

Whatever the truth of the matter, school uniforms, at present, remain very much part of schooling in England.

Formal language

When writing a formal piece of writing, you would usually use impersonal language although this depends on the **audience** and **purpose**.

Whenever you sit down to write, you must think **who** (audience) and **why** (purpose), as this will then shape the style and content of the writing.

For instance if you are asked to write a letter you need to think:

- **Who** (audience)?

  Formal = headteacher, adult you do not know well, company...

  Informal = friend, family member you know well...

- **Why** (purpose)?

  Formal = an apology, an introduction, a complaint...

  Informal = your news, about a holiday, thank you for a present...

Top Tip

Always read your writing back to check that it is the same style throughout.

Key words

impersonal

formal

third person

Quick test

Would your writing be personal or impersonal for the following scenarios?

1. A postcard from holiday to a friend
2. A letter to a company about a product
3. A biography about a famous person
4. Speech between friends in a story
5. A note to your mum about where you are

Test practice questions

1 You are looking over your work and decide to replace the word **'happy'** in the sentence below.

The girl was happy that she had won the race.

Choose another word with a similar meaning and write it in the box.

| |
| |

1 mark

2 Draw lines to join the antonyms to their partners.

happy		sad

dark		hard

soft		light

1 mark

3 You are looking over your work and decide to replace the word **'nice'** in the sentence below.

The boy said that his present was nice.

Choose another word with a similar meaning and write it in the box.

| |
| |

1 mark

1 Draw lines to match each phrase to the correct writer's technique.

The hog and frog sat on the log		onomatopoeia

Five fat frogs		assonance

SPLAT!		alliteration

1 mark

2 You are looking over your work and decide to replace the word 'said' in the sentence below.

"This lesson is so boring!" said Megan to Josh, who was sitting next to her.

Choose a suitable word and write it in the box.

1 mark

3 Complete the table by inserting a **synonym** and an **antonym**.

Word	Synonym	Antonym
kind		
hot		

1 mark

4 Finish the sentence using personification for imagery.

The waves _____ **1 mark**

Answers

Grammar

PAGES 4–5 NOUNS AND PRONOUNS
1 proper   **2** collective   **3** common
4 abstract   **5** proper

PAGES 6–7 VERBS AND ADVERBS
1 past   **2** present
3 past   **4** future

PAGES 8–9 ADJECTIVES
1 <u>fastest</u> – superlative
2 <u>beautiful</u> – adjective
3 <u>slower</u> – comparative
4 <u>soft</u> – adjective

PAGES 10–11 SUBJECT–VERB AGREEMENT
1 The <u>letters</u> (were flying) through the letterbox.
2 The <u>letter</u> (flew) through the letterbox.

PAGES 12–13 CONNECTIVES
1 <u>because</u>   **2** <u>before</u>
3 <u>otherwise</u>   **4** <u>as a result of</u>

PAGES 14–15 TYPES OF SENTENCE
For example:
1 To scare the man, the lion roared loudly.
2 The children ran away because they were scared.
3 The snow, that was glistening white, fell gently.

PAGES 16–17 COMPLEX SENTENCES
1 Because they were cold, <u>the children put their coats on.</u>
2 <u>The girl,</u> who had red hair, <u>climbed the steps of the slide.</u>
3 <u>The monkeys,</u> who made a lot of noise, <u>swung from the trees,</u> because they were showing off.
4 After a very long drive, <u>the family arrived at their destination!</u>
5 Even though it was late, <u>Harry walked to the shops</u> as he wanted some chocolate.

PAGES 18–19 PREPOSITIONS AND ARTICLES
1 <u>in</u>
2 <u>on</u>
3 <u>into</u>
4 <u>above</u>
5 <u>over</u>

PAGES 20–21 PARAGRAPHS
Independent task. Children should note that paragraph changes are used for action, characters, setting changes, etc. Linking words should also be noted.

PAGES 22–23 TENSE AGREEMENT
1 future   **2** present (continuous)
3 past   **4** present   **5** past

PAGES 24–25 ACTIVE AND PASSIVE VOICE
1 passive   **2** passive   **3** active
4 active   **5** passive   **6** active

PAGES 26–27 PRECISION IN VOCABULARY
For example:
1 I had a great time last night with my friends.
2 I am not going to work hard anymore.
3 I know that I should not have done it.

PAGES 28–31 TEST PRACTICE QUESTIONS
Level 3 questions
1 **a)** are **b)** ran **c)** were [1 mark: all 3 correct for 1 mark]
2 For example: I love playing in the park with my friends.
[1 mark]
3

Word from the sentence	Noun	Adjective
lesson	✓	
boring		✓
Matilda	✓	

[1 mark: all 3 correct for 1 mark]
4 Maxwell wanted a dog; <u>he</u> had always longed for a dog but <u>his</u> parents would not allow <u>him</u> to have <u>one</u>. [2 marks: 1 mark for 3 correct, 2 marks for all correct]
5 skipped – verb; merrily – adverb; road – noun [1 mark: all 3 correct for 1 mark]

Level 4 questions
1 The children ran (up) the hill and then they jumped (over) the fence!
[1 mark: both correct for 1 mark]

2

	Main clause	Subordinate clause
My mum, who looks after me very well, **always nags me to tidy my room.**	✓	
The police came to the house because the owners phoned them.	✓	
The computer, **which is brand new,** has stopped working!		✓

[1 mark: all correct for 1 mark]

3 A C B A **[1 mark: all correct for 1 mark]**

4 (Despite) the bad weather, the show had to go on! **[1 mark]**

5 The loudest dog (was) the prettiest **[1 mark]**

Level 5 questions

1 The man put an umbrella up as the rain started to fall ☑ **[1 mark]**

2 Although there was fire damage, <u>the school was open to children</u>. **[1 mark]**

3 despite **[1 mark]**

4 a) B **b)** A **c)** A **[2 marks: 1 mark for 2 correct, 2 marks for all 3 correct]**

Level 6 questions

1 The letter to parents was written by the headteacher ☑ **[1 mark]**

2

	Adverb of time	Adverb of place	Adverb of manner	Adverb of frequency
yesterday	✓			
occasionally				✓
quietly			✓	
inside		✓		

[1 mark: all correct for 1 mark]

3 For example: The children played happily in the park and then they went home. **[1 mark]**

4 PR, CL, CM, AB **[1 mark: all correct for 1 mark]**

5 have; is; work **[1 mark: all correct for 1 mark]**

Punctuation

PAGES 32–33 FULL STOPS, CAPITAL LETTERS AND MORE

1 ? **2** ! **3** .

4 . **5** !

PAGES 34–35 COMMAS, COLONS AND SEMI-COLONS

1 The teacher said we needed: pens, pencils, rubbers and crayons.

2 Despite the sunshine, the ground was still wet.

3 Mary, who was very fit, ran in the London marathon.

PAGES 36–37 INVERTED COMMAS

For example:

1 The man asked for some help to buy some chocolate.

2 The lady screamed about the mess when she walked into the kitchen.

3 The policeman asked the suspect to think more carefully about where he had been the night before.

4 Sophie said that she was excited about being in the swimming gala at the weekend.

5 Mary asked her dad where they were going.

PAGES 38–39 APOSTROPHES

1 omission / contraction

2 possession

3 omission / contraction

4 omission / contraction

5 possession

PAGES 40–41 BRACKETS AND DASHES

1 The man was staring thoughtfully at the house – I didn't know him.

2 Buckingham Palace (where the Queen lives) is in London.

3 The new houses – six bungalows and two blocks of flats – were opened this morning. **[Brackets would also be accepted here]**

4 The man crept through the door – he came face to face with a bear!

PAGES 42–43 HYPHENS AND ELLIPSIS

For example:

1 ice: -skate, -skating, -skater, -palace

2 twenty: -three, -five-, -seven

3 mid: -point, -September,

4 spot: -light, -check

PAGES 44-45 FULL USE OF PUNCTUATION
Children's own answers

PAGES 46-49 TEST PRACTICE QUESTIONS
Level 3 questions
1 It is going to be my birthday in May. I am going to invite all of my friends to my party. **[1 mark: a semi-colon would also be accepted here]**
2 How many times have you been to France – ?
   Wow, that's amazing – !
   I have green eyes – . **[1 mark: all 3 correct for 1 mark]**
3 For example: Where are my shoes? **[1 mark]**
4 I had to pack: shirts, trousers, socks and pants. ☑ **[1 mark]**

Level 4 questions
1 The man stopped, looked intently at the floor, then hurried on. ☑ **[1 mark]**
2 I have to take a rucksack, a sleeping bag, a torch, biscuits and a warm hat. **[1 mark]**
3 For example: Matthew said, "I'm going on holiday to Spain in the summer." **[1 mark]**
4

	Apostrophe for omission	Apostrophe for possession
It's still raining outside.	✓	
They're all waiting for the bus!	✓	
It was Max's turn next.		✓

[1 mark: all correct for 1 mark]

Level 5 questions
1 a) brackets
   b) To add additional information ☑
      [1 mark: both correct for 1 mark]
2 The TV presenter announced that the winner was ... Bob the Builder! **[1 mark]**
   ☑
3 Tower Bridge (which was built between 1886 and 1894) spans the River Thames. ☑
   [1 mark]

Level 6 questions
1 I need to buy: bread (wholemeal), milk (semi-skimmed) and butter. **[1 mark]**
2 The sun is shining brightly in the sky; I will invite my friends for a barbecue. **[1 mark]**
3 we have – we've
   we will – we'll
   we did – we'd **[1 mark: all 3 correct for 1 mark]**
4 For example: David told his mother that he would not be able to visit her at the weekend as he was going to a concert. **[1 mark]**
5 We'll have to go and own up that we damaged Scott's car. **[1 mark]**

Spelling

PAGES 50-51 PREFIXES AND SUFFIXES
For example:
1 malnourish; nourishment / nourishing
2 mislead; leading / leader
3 intake; taking / taken
4 hyperactive; actively / activate

PAGES 52-53 MORE COMPLEX PREFIXES AND SUFFIXES
For example:
1 art of healing
2 not
3 in a direction of manner
4 other

PAGES 54-55 VOWELS AND CONSONANTS
For example:
1 hair, help, hotel, happy
2 centre, cellar, cinema, send, sand
3 day, dark, dentist, deer
4 cake, kind, sky, break

PAGES 56-57 HOMOPHONES AND HOMONYMS
For example:
1 sale: the action of selling something;
   sail: a piece of material on a mast to catch the wind

2 beach: a pebbly or sandy short by the sea; beech: a large tree

3 wait: remain where one is; weight: an item's relative mass

4 key: a small piece of metal shaped to fit in a keyhole; quay: a platform lying alongside water for loading/unloading ships

5 tale: a story; tail: the rear-end of an animal that sticks out from the rest of the body

PAGES 58-59 SPELLING STRATEGIES 1
Children's own spelling words to be revised.

PAGES 60-61 SPELLING STRATEGIES 2
Children's own black list of spelling words.

PAGES 62-63 WORD FAMILIES, ROOTS AND ORIGINS
1 skill **2** contrary
3 between **4** many **5** across

PAGES 64-65 MORE COMPLEX WORD FAMILIES
For example:
1 glass, pane, double-glazed, transparent, shiny
2 office, work, table, paper, wooden
3 machine, mouse, keyboard, memory, screen
4 reflection, shiny, looking glass, reflect, image

PAGES 66-67 INFLECTIONAL ENDINGS
1 meddled
2 tugged
3 hurried
4 looked
5 grinned

PAGES 68-69 EDITING SKILLS
For example:
Emily walked to work slowly and thoughtfully; if only she had a car. Her feet always hurt by the end of the day from all the walking. She was going to buy a car. But where would she get the money?

PAGES 70-73 TEST PRACTICE QUESTIONS
Level 3 questions
1 pairs; their; too **[1 mark: all correct for 1 mark]**
2 business **[1 mark]**
3 ad- **[1 mark]**
4 **For example:** suddenly, hopefully; rained, gained **[1 mark: all correct for 1 mark]**

Level 4 questions
1 a)–b) For example: a movement of the hand from left to right as a greeting / a long body of water that curls over **[1 mark]**

2 The jewellery box lives on my special shelf in my bedroom. **[1 mark]**

3

Word	One syllable	Two syllables	Three syllables
helpful		✓	
hopefully			✓
fruit	✓		
pencil		✓	

[1 mark: all correct for 1 mark]
4 helped **[1 mark]**
5 **For example:** aquamarine, aquarium, aqualung, aquatics **[1 mark: 3 correct for 1 mark]**

Level 5 questions
1

	add 'd'	double the final consonant before adding -ed	add -ed
help			✓
trudge	✓		
shame	✓		
hop		✓	

[1 mark: all correct for 1 mark]
2 **dis**-prove; **un**-attractive; **mis**-trust **[1 mark]**
3 ring **[1 mark]**

Level 6 questions
1 **For example:** unhappy, unlikely, unhelpful **[1 mark]**
2 suitable; foreign **[1 mark]**
3 writer/writing; creator/creating **[1 mark]**
4 medicine, biology, astronaut **[1 mark]**
5

	un-	dis-	mal-	im-
-personal				✓
-necessary	✓			
-advantage		✓		
-nutrition			✓	
-patient				✓

[2 marks: award 1 mark for 3 or 4 correct and 2 marks for all 5 correct]

Vocabulary

PAGES 74-75 ANTONYMS AND SYNONYMS
1 closed
2 cold
3 small / little
4 girl
5 pull
6 loud

PAGES 76-77 SPEECH VOCABULARY
For example:
1 "I am going to retire at the end of the year," said the teacher.
2 "My smile has slipped from my face!" joked the clown.
3 "My knowledge of grammar has improved," remarked Nancy.
4 "Help! Help!" shouted the lady.
5 James whined, "How much further is the journey going to be?"

PAGES 78-79 SINGULAR AND PLURAL
1 tables
2 ladies
3 coats
4 calves
5 cargoes

PAGES 80-81 TECHNICAL VOCABULARY
1 A large building where town business was dealt with
2 A cart with two wheels which was pulled by horses. Romans raced chariots.
3 A system of pipes and channels which brought clean water into towns
4 Roman central heating – hot air flowed through gaps between walls and floors
5 The Roman government
6 A metal pen for scratching words into wax on wooden tablets.

PAGES 82-83 FIGURATIVE LANGUAGE
1 onomatopoeia
2 personification
3 alliteration
4 metaphor
5 assonance

PAGES 84-85 PERSONAL FORM AND IMPERSONAL FORM
1 personal
2 impersonal
3 impersonal
4 personal
5 personal

PAGES 86-87 TEST PRACTICE QUESTIONS
Level 3 and 4 questions
1 **For example:** glad, proud, pleased, excited **[1 mark]**
2 happy – sad; dark – light; soft – hard **[1 mark: all correct for 1 mark]**
3 **For example:** lovely, great, fantastic, good, fine **[1 mark]**

Level 5 and 6 questions
1 The hog and frog sat on the log – assonance; Five fat frogs – alliteration; SPLAT! – onomatopoeia **[1 mark: all correct for 1 mark]**
2 **For example:** whispered, exclaimed, moaned **[1 mark]**
3

Word	Synonym	Antonym
kind	caring / nice	unkind / mean
hot	warm / boiling / fiery	cold

[1 mark]
4 **For example:** The waves danced across the shore / the waves scampered… **[1 mark]**

abstract noun – a noun that generally describes things that exist but cannot be seen, heard, smelt, felt or tasted

active voice – where the subject of the sentence is doing the action

adjective – a word that describes a noun

adverb – a word that tells us more about a verb (or sometimes other words)

alliteration – when a sound is repeated at the start of words

antonym – a word that is opposite in meaning to another word

apostrophe – a punctuation mark used to signal a missing letter or the ownership of something

article – 'the', 'a' and 'an' are the articles in the English language

assonance – where vowel sounds are repeated in the middle of words

bracket – a punctuation mark used to enclose words to separate them from the main part of the text

capital letter – an uppercase letter used at the beginning of sentences, for the pronoun 'I' and at the start of proper nouns

clause – a part of a sentence that contains a subject and a verb but does not have to make sense on its own

collective noun – a name that refers to a group or collection of people or things

colloquialisms – informal language used mainly in speech

colon – a quotation mark used before a list, quotation or explanation

comma – a punctuation mark representing a short pause in a sentence, or to separate items in a list

command – a sentence that gives an order or instruction

common noun – a noun that names a kind of person or thing

comparative adjective – an adjective that compares one thing with another (usually with the ending 'er')

complex sentence – a sentence that is made up of a main clause and one or more subordinate clauses

compound sentence – a sentence that is made up of two or more equally weighted simple sentences joined by a connective, semi-colon or colon

connective – a word or phrase used to join clauses or sentences

consonant – any letter of the alphabet that is not a vowel

continuous tense – the tense that is used to show that something is happening for a while

contraction – a shortened form of two words using an apostrophe

dash – a punctuation mark that marks a pause or a break in the sense of the text

definite article – 'the' is the only definite article in the English language

direct speech – speech that is used to show the exact words spoken in inverted commas

editing – the review and correction of text

ellipsis – a punctuation mark that is a series of three dots, usually indicating an omission of a word, sentence or section. It can also be used to indicate an unfinished thought or a trailing off into silence

exclamation – a sentence that expresses a strong emotion

exclamation mark – a punctuation mark used at the end of a word, phrase or sentence to indicate strong feelings or high volume

figurative language – words (or phrases) that change or exaggerate the actual meaning of the words, e.g. metaphors, similes and personification

formal language – the conventional use of language in a standard form

form-based – a word family formed from words that have a common root word or letter string

full stop – the strongest punctuation mark as it indicates the end of a sentence that is not a question or exclamation

future tense – this locates an action as going to happen (in the future)

glossary – a collection of useful words and their meanings, often showing technical vocabulary

homonym – a word that is spelt the same but has more than one meaning

homophone – a word that sounds the same as another word but is spelt differently

hyphen – a punctuation mark used to link two or more words together to make one word or expression

impersonal language – the language used in formal writing or speech

indefinite article – 'a' and 'an' are the indefinite articles in the English language

inflectional ending – a common ending added to a root word

inverted comma – a punctuation mark used to show the exact words that someone has spoken (also referred to as a speech mark or quotation)

main clause – the main part of the sentence that makes sense on its own

meaning-based – a word family formed from words that relate in meaning but not in form

metaphor – when something is described as if it were something else

mnemonics – making silly sentences or words to help you remember spellings

omission – a shortened form of two words using an apostrophe

onomatopoeia – a word that sounds the same as the thing that it is describing

origin – the language / place from where a word has come from

paragraph – a group of sentences linked together by a common theme

passive voice – where the object is doing the action

past tense – this locates an action as having already happened (in the past)

personification – when an object or thing is given human qualities

phrase – a group of words not built around a verb / a part of a sentence

plural – more than one of something

possession – when someone owns something

prefix – a group of letters added to the beginning of a word to change its meaning

preposition – a word used for showing what one noun has to do with another, usually where they are in relation to each other

present tense – this locates an action as happening now (in the present)

pronoun – a word which is used instead of a noun

proper noun – a noun that refers to a particular person, place or thing

punctuation – marks that give sense and meaning to text

question – a sentence that is worded in order to find out information

question mark – a punctuation mark used at the end of a sentence that asks a question

repetition – repeating previously used language

reported speech – when we are told what somebody has said rather than the words actually spoken

root word – the base part of a word which carries most of the meaning

semi-colon – a punctuation mark used for joining two related sentences or to separate items in a complex list

sentence – a set of words that is complete in itself (it always contains a verb and usually a subject)

simile – when one thing is compared to another, using the words 'like' or 'as'

simple sentence – a sentence with only one clause containing a subject and verb

singular – one of something

slang – informal language used mainly in speech

speech mark – a punctuation mark used to show the exact words that someone has spoken

spelling – the correct order of letters in a word

Standard English – when all the rules of the English language are correctly applied to speech or writing

statement – a sentence that declares information

subject – the person or thing doing the action in the sentence

subordinate clause – a clause which adds extra information to the main clause, but does not make sense on its own

suffix – a letter or group of letters added to the end of a word to change the way you use it

superlative adjective – an adjective that is used to show that one noun is different from all the others

syllable – a unit of sound containing a single vowel sound, with or without consonants

synonym – a word that is similar in meaning to another and can be used to avoid repeating the same word throughout a piece of writing

technical vocabulary – words that are associated with a particular content area or topic

tense – shows whether something has happened, is happening or is going to happen

third person – a narrative written format using 'he', 'she',' it' or 'they'

topic sentence – a sentence in a paragraph (usually at the start) that summarises the key information

verb – a word which shows some kind of action or being

vowel – there are five vowels in the alphabet (a, e, i, o, u)

word family – groups of words that derive from the same root words

Acknowledgements

Cover ©hellbilly, ©Petr Vaclavek; P01 ©hellbilly; P04 ©Klara Viskova, ©Pixel Embargo, ©Naia, ©Virinaflora; P05 ©korinoxe, ©Hermin; P06 ©pichayasri, ©ativka@mail.ru; P08 ©Solomin Andrey; P09 ©Memo Angeles; P10 ©SASIMOTO, ©zzveillust; P 12 ©Matthew Cole; P13 ©Primusoid; P14 ©Memo Angeles; P18 ©Art Painter; P19 ©Cyborgwitch; P20 Mike McDonald; P21 ©Memo Angeles; P34 ©89studio; P41 ©Studio Barcelona; P42 ©Itana, ©Alhovik; P44 ©Motimo; P51 ©losw;

P52 ©RAStudio, ©Aleksangel; P55 ©pockygallery, ©LoopAll, ©Dragana Gerasimoski; P56 ©insima, ©Kynata, ©Sashkin, ©SlipFloat; P57 ©svkv, ©Dan Gerber, ©James Steidl, ©williammpark, ©Sergey Furtaev, ©Hibrida, ©olegtoka, ©TDay, ©stiven; P60 ©Klara Viskova; P62 ©Rinslet; P63 ©Chuhail; P64 ©zzveillust, ©la Kwasniewski; P65 ©zzveillust, ©Matthew Cole, ©dedMazay, ©Jan Hyrman; P67 ©Zand; P69 ©Malchev; P74 Ela Kwasniewski; P75 Knumina Studios;

P77 ©Amornism; P78 ©jehsomwang; P79 ©sergey titov; ©Willierossin; P80 ©Naci Yavuz, ©Merkushev Vasiliy, ©Milagli; P82 ©CarpathianPrince; P83 ©antipathique, ©Tribalium, ©softRobot; P85 ©mexrix, ©lineartestpilot. All images above are used under license from Shutterstock.com

P65 ©istockphoto.com/Todd Harrison

All other images are ©Jupiterimages or Letts Educational, an imprint of HarperCollins*Publishers*